1787	A second edition of **Poems, Chiefly in the Scottish Dialect** is published in Edinburgh
	Burns meets Agnes McLehose, better known as 'Clarinda'
	Burns meets James Johnson and agrees to contribute to **The Scots Musical Museum**
	Burns tours the Highlands, Stirlingshire and the Borders, collecting local songs and airs
1788	Burns's marriage to Jean Armour is officially recognised by the Kirk
	Burns takes on the lease of Ellisland Farm, near Dumfries
1789	Struggling to make the farm pay, Burns begins work as an Excise officer
1790	Burns writes **Tam o' Shanter**, recalling the places of his childhood in Alloway
1791	Burns and his family move to Dumfries
1792	Burns is promoted within the Excise to the Port Division in Dumfries
	Burns begins work on **A Select Collection of Original Scotish Airs for the Voice** with George Thomson
1793–5	Burns writes, amongst other songs, **Auld lang syne**, **Scots wha hae** and **A man's a man for a' that**
1796	Burns dies in Dumfries on 21 July, aged 37
	On the day of his funeral, Jean gives birth to the couple's fifth son
1797	The first biography of Burns is published
1801	The first 'Burns Supper' to commemorate the poet is held in the cottage at Alloway
1815	Burns's coffin is moved to its present resting place in the mausoleum in St Michael's Kirkyard, Dumfries. His wife Jean, who survived him by 38 years, and five of their nine children are buried with him
1823	Burns Monument, located in the poet's birthplace of Alloway, opens to the public. It becomes a place of pilgrimage for Burns's admirers and a focus for events celebrating his life and work

CONTENTS

FOREWORD

STEWART CONN,
POET AND PLAYWRIGHT

From **Tam o' Shanter**
to his epistles and love
lyrics Burns transformed
poetry in Scots. The
songs which were the
late flowering of his
genius preserved and
enriched Scotland's
folk tradition and now
resonate world-wide:
Bob Dylan has claimed
that **A red red rose** was
the main source of his creative inspiration –
and what could be more universal than
Auld lang syne?

Burns's nationalism was international,
embracing a belief in the dignity of man. The
idealism of **A man's a man for a' that**, sung at
the relaunch of Scotland's Parliament, retains
its urgency, as do the vitality and satirical
wit with which he lambasted hypocrisy and
the unco guid. Fame did not make him lose
the common touch or sever himself from his
peasant roots.

He has survived bowdlerisation, the more
mawkish aspects of the Burns Supper cult
and the hazard of being all things to all men.
Many of his phrases are in everyday usage
while his language of the heart, imbued with
compassion and a sense of transience, has
entered our bloodstream.

At last, in his birthplace, we can hail Burns's
unrivalled achievement and renown, and fully
savour the interplay between him and the
Ayrshire soil he sprang from.

THE ALLOWAY YEARS

Robert Burns's parents came from a long line of farmers. His father, William Burnes, hailed from the north-east of Scotland and his mother, Agnes, was brought up on a farm near Kirkoswald in south Ayrshire. At the age of twelve, following the death of her own mother, Agnes was sent to live with her maternal grandmother. The Scottish songs and ballads she probably learned from her grandmother stayed with Agnes all her life. At the age of 25, Agnes met and fell in love with William Burnes, a gardener eleven years her senior.

As a young man William Burnes had trained and worked as a landscape gardener. By 1754, aged 33, he was practising his trade on an estate near Alloway. Unmarried, he lived a frugal life, sending regular funds for the upkeep of his elderly, impoverished father. Around this time, his father died and William was free to plan for his own future. He set his sights on starting his own market garden, growing fruit and vegetables for sale, and it was with this in mind that he bought the land at Alloway, naming it 'New Gardens' to reflect his ambitions.

In the 1750s Alloway was a tiny hamlet, set in the open countryside of Kyle, on the Ayrshire coast. The site which William acquired was on a gentle slope leading down to Sergeant's Burn. It was here that he started to build a two-roomed cottage, while still working as a gardener on a nearby estate. His son Gilbert later recalled:

'At length, being desirous to settle in life, he took a perpetual lease of some acres of land from Dr Campbell, physician in Ayr, with a view to cultivate it as a nursery and meal-garden. With his own hands he built a house on part of this ground ...'

(Letter from Gilbert Burns to Mrs Frances Anna Dunlop, 1797)

In 1756 William went to the Maybole Fair where he met Agnes Broun. The couple married the following year and Agnes came to live at the cottage in Alloway. William's plans for his market garden proved difficult to achieve: he was so tied up working as a gardener on neighbouring estates that he had little time to invest in his own land. Instead, Agnes took over the running of the land, turning it into a small farm or smallholding. Much of the land became pasture for cows which Agnes milked, making butter and cheese to sell at market. The family grew crops to sell, including corn which they may have threshed in the barn. Close to the cottage William laid out a kailyard (kitchen garden) where Agnes grew kale, potatoes and probably leeks, carrots and onions to feed the couple's growing family.

Background on main photo: detail from a certificate confirming William Burnes's good character, issued by his employers Sir William Ogilvy and John Stewart

hn Stewart of Futhie do hereby certifie
declare that the bearer William Burness
the Son of an honest Farmer in this
ighbourhood, & is a very well inclin
ad himself. We therefore recom
ny Nobleman or Gentlem
o far as he is Capable
nd

The cottage that William
built still stands today.
This is where Robert Burns
was born and lived until
the age of seven.

'THERE WAS A LAD WAS BORN IN KYLE'

Four months after she married William Burnes, Agnes became pregnant. On 25 January 1759, attended by the blacksmith's wife, Agnes gave birth to Robert in the box bed in the kitchen of the cottage at Alloway. Like many new parents, Agnes and William Burnes must have held their new-born son and dreamed of his future. Little could they have imagined that their tiny infant would grow up to become Scotland's national poet, celebrated the world over.

When the baby was only a week old, a ferocious storm damaged the cottage, destroying part of the roof and gable-end. So severe was the damage that Agnes and her baby son had to seek shelter with a neighbour while the house was repaired.

Main picture: the box bed in the cottage where Robert and three of his siblings were born

Above, from left: Burns Cottage; small milking stool said to have belonged to the Burns family; eighteenth-century and replica horn cups – cups made of cow horn would have been readily available to country folk, and Burns would have drunk from cups like these

In keeping with tradition, Robert was named after his paternal grandfather, Robert Burnes. The family also sometimes used the spelling 'Burness' for their surname. But by 1786, when his first book of poetry was published, Robert had changed the spelling to Burns. He may simply have removed the unused letters because the name was pronounced 'Burns' in Ayrshire.

Robert Burns.

Our monarch's hindmost year but *ane*   one
Was five-and-twenty days begun,
'Twas then a blast o' Janwar' Win'
Blew *hansel* in on Robin.   gift

RANTIN' ROVIN' ROBIN (1787)

ROBERT'S EARLY YEARS

He'll hae misfortunes great and sma',
But ay a heart *aboon* them a';   *above*
He'll be a credit till us a',
We'll a' be proud o' Robin.

RANTIN' ROVIN' ROBIN (1787)

8

By the time Robert was 20 months old, his brother Gilbert had arrived. In the years that followed, two sisters (Agnes and Anabella) were born at the cottage, and Agnes and William would go on to have another three children at Mount Oliphant Farm, their next home. All seven children survived to maturity, which is remarkable at a time of high infant mortality.

Robert's parents were strict, industrious, religious and loving. As the eldest son, Robert was expected to help his parents, as well as entertain the ever-growing band of younger siblings. With less than two years between them, Robert and Gilbert formed a strong relationship. From a young age the boys were assigned household chores, which included feeding and looking after the family's cows, horse and chickens and helping with threshing corn. Being the eldest also brought privileges, as Robert and Gilbert were allowed to accompany their father to market.

When the children were not employed in family duties, they had time to play. The countryside surrounding the cottage made a wonderful playground with space to run free, guddle in the burns and watch wildlife in the woods and hills surrounding the River Doon. Just outside the cottage, the main road running from Ayr to Maybole carried a regular passage of travellers, coaches and carriages, providing an endless source of entertainment for the young Burnes children.

Robert's upbringing and childhood experiences at Alloway helped to shape his character and fire his interests, and would influence his work in later life.

FAMILY TREE

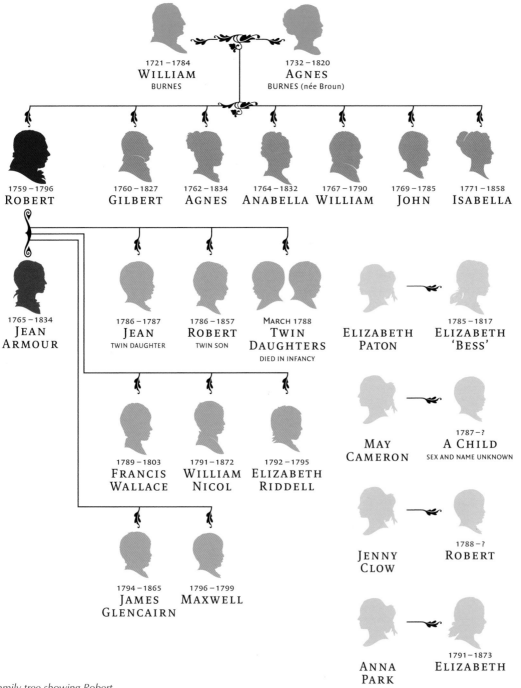

1721 – 1784
WILLIAM
BURNES

1732 – 1820
AGNES
BURNES (née Broun)

1759 – 1796
ROBERT

1760 – 1827
GILBERT

1762 – 1834
AGNES

1764 – 1832
ANABELLA

1767 – 1790
WILLIAM

1769 – 1785
JOHN

1771 – 1858
ISABELLA

1765 – 1834
JEAN ARMOUR

1786 – 1787
JEAN
TWIN DAUGHTER

1786 – 1857
ROBERT
TWIN SON

MARCH 1788
TWIN DAUGHTERS
DIED IN INFANCY

ELIZABETH PATON

1785 – 1817
ELIZABETH 'BESS'

1789 – 1803
FRANCIS WALLACE

1791 – 1872
WILLIAM NICOL

1792 – 1795
ELIZABETH RIDDELL

MAY CAMERON

1787 – ?
A CHILD
SEX AND NAME UNKNOWN

1794 – 1865
JAMES GLENCAIRN

1796 – 1799
MAXWELL

JENNY CLOW

1788 – ?
ROBERT

ANNA PARK

1791 – 1873
ELIZABETH

Family tree showing Robert and his siblings; his children by his wife Jean Armour; and his children by other women

O, YE, whose cheek the tear of pity stains,
Draw near with pious reverence and attend
Here lie the loving husband's dear remains,
The tender father, and the generous friend;
The pitying heart that felt for human woe,
The dauntless heart that fear'd no human pride;
The friend of man, to vice alone a foe,
"For ev'n his failings lean'd to virtue's side."

11

Burns Cottage

Painting of Burns Cottage by John Fleming, 1816. It shows an extension built on the left of the original cottage, which converted it for use as an alehouse during the nineteenth century

The cottage at Alloway would initially have been a 'but and ben' design: two rooms divided by a bed and partition. The family lived in one room, dry and warm with the comfort of a fire for heat and cooking; the animals were next door, their smell, sweat and warmth forming the odorous backdrop to daily life.

When Robert was growing up, the relationship between man and animal was totally interdependent. Animals were not viewed in the modern-day sense as a 'crop' to be consumed, but kept instead for milk, eggs, wool and strength to pull the plough. They were slaughtered only if they were ill or unable to survive the winter, and occasionally for a feast or celebration. From his earliest days Robert was taught respect and compassion for animals, which remained with him throughout his life.

As the family grew, William Burnes probably extended the cottage, adding a byre and a barn.

The kitchen was where day-to-day life took place. Here, the family slept in box beds, dressed and undressed, cooked on the range, ate, drank, talked, sang and made music sitting around the fire.

The spence (or parlour) was the more formal room and afforded the great luxury of some domestic privacy. This was probably the room where Robert and Gilbert were sometimes taught, where their father would read the Bible to the family and where they would pray together. The spence would also have been a work space for Agnes's dairy.

In the evenings, the cottage was lit by candles and crusie oil lamps. As peat burned in the fire and candles cast long shadows, young Robert would sit listening to the songs, music, stories and gossip of his family and friends.

A well to the south-west of the cottage provided essential water for washing and cooking.

The kitchen at Burns Cottage; parts of the dresser are thought to be original to the cottage

SEEDS OF INSPIRATION

STORIES AND SUPERSTITION

By the time Robert was six, the small cottage was home to his mother, father, brother Gilbert, two younger sisters and a cousin of his mother's called Betty Davidson. In return for her board and lodging, Betty helped about the house and in the dairy. For Robert, Betty's influence was far-reaching:

'In my infant and boyish days too, I owed much to an old Maid of my Mother's, remarkable for her ignorance, credulity and superstition. She had, I suppose, the largest collection in the county of tales and songs concerning devils, ghosts, fairies, brownies, witches, warlocks ...'

(Letter from Robert Burns to Dr John Moore, 2 August 1787)

ALLOWAY AULD KIRK

The Auld Kirk bears a date suggesting it was built in 1516, but parts of it may date back as early as the thirteenth century. By the 1740s, the church was also being used as a school, but a decade later it lay deserted and eventually fell into a state of disrepair. On the initiative of William Burnes, the villagers made some attempt to tidy up the graveyard, but the church remained ruinous and deserted. It was this empty ruin which became 'Alloway's Auld Haunted Kirk' in the mind of the young Robert.

Superstition was a potent force within Alloway's rural culture. Fear of the Devil, Hell and its associated demons was very real and formed the stuff of 'idle terrors' for Robert as a child. Just along the road from the Burnes family cottage stood Alloway Auld Kirk. Surrounded by its graveyard full of ancient gravestones, it was an eerie place populated in Robert's mind by ghosts and other supernatural creatures. One event that fired his imagination as a child was the account of a stray Highland bullock that wandered into the old roofless kirk and became trapped without food or water. A few days later, a local woman passing by saw the horned head staring at her through the open church window. As the beast let out a huge bellow, the woman fled in terror believing that she had seen the Devil in the Auld Kirk. Like many events in his childhood, this story stayed with Robert and would later play its role in one of his most famous poems, **Tam o' Shanter**.

Witches and Warlocks in a Dance by Alexander Goudie (1933–2004). Goudie created a series of 54 paintings illustrating scenes from Tam o' Shanter, *now on permanent public display in Rozelle House, near Alloway*

In 1784 when the poet's father died, his body was brought back from Tarbolton, where the family were living, to be buried in the graveyard of the Auld Kirk at Alloway. In a poignant tribute, Robert penned an epitaph for his father, which was inscribed on his gravestone. The original manuscript (right) ends with the lines:

The friend of man, to Vice alone a foe;
"For even his failings lean'd to Virtue's side."

INSPIRED BY FORMAL LEARNING

One of the greatest influences in Robert's early life was his father and his enlightened views on education. William Burnes believed in the merits of education for its own sake as well as for advancement in life. He also regarded the religious instruction of his children as being of the utmost importance.

At the beginning of 1765, when Robert was aged six, a new school opened at nearby Alloway Mill. Here, Robert and Gilbert were sent to learn the basics of reading and writing. It was, however, a short-lived experience, for within a matter of weeks the schoolmaster relocated and the school closed. William was determined to secure an education for his children and engaged nineteen-year-old John Murdoch to teach them.

Robert's early schooling gave him a taste for literature, which stirred in him a sense of pride in his Scottish identity. Some years later he wrote:

Soon after Robert's birth, William began work on a theological book for the religious guidance of his offspring, later published as A Manual of Religious Belief

'The two first books I ever read in private, and which gave me more pleasure than any two books I ever read again, were, the life of Hannibal and the history of Sir William Wallace ... the story of Wallace poured a Scotish prejudice in my veins which will boil along there till the flood-gates of life shut in eternal rest.'

(Letter from Robert Burns to Dr John Moore, 2 August 1787)

That 'Scotish prejudice' would also manifest itself in a Scottish pride, and came to the fore in later life when he wrote such works as **Scots wha hae** and **Such a parcel of rogues in a nation**.

Burns and his brother *by William Hill Thomson (1882–1956)*

BURNS'S SCHOOLING

PROFESSOR ROBERT CRAWFORD,
UNIVERSITY OF ST ANDREWS

Burns's most important early education came from his mother's side of the family through sung Scots songs and spoken Scots folktales. Yet English language reading was also essential to him as a writer. The words 'William Burnes g[ardener] at Alloa' in the 'List of the subscribers for Mr Stackhouse's history of the Bible', published in Kilmarnock in 1765, is one of many reminders that Burns's father was eager to have improving books in the Alloway household. Burns remembered Stackhouse's book from childhood. In 1765 Burns's father hired John Murdoch, a young schoolteacher from Ayr to tutor five local families. Burns's father spoke unusually correct English. He wanted his sons to be able to do likewise, so Robert read examples of good English style such as Joseph Addison's *Spectator* magazine. Like William Burnes, John Murdoch linked 'love of VIRTUE' with educational 'REGULARITY, ORDER or METHOD'. His pupils read the Bible and Arthur Masson's *Collection of English Prose and Verse* alongside an *English Grammar*. Murdoch thought Robert's musical 'ear … was remarkably dull, and his voice untunable', but from Murdoch Burns learned a lot.

Burns was excited by writings in Masson's collection by Addison, James Thomson, Alexander Pope and others. Murdoch lent Burns a biography of Hannibal, and Burns enjoyed the story of the North African rebel who fought Roman imperialism; soon after, he delighted in tales of Scottish freedom-fighter William Wallace. Murdoch's teaching quickened in Burns a lifelong love of reading. Though his regular schooling with Murdoch was interrupted at the age of nine, his father went on encouraging him. Murdoch gave the family books such as Shakespeare's *Titus Andronicus* (whose bloodthirsty violence disgusted young Robert) and a comic play about how to 'act the lover', translated from French as *The School for Lovers*, which the nine-year-old lapped up.

Murdoch Instructing Burns *by George Washington Brownlow, 1859*

A little later, Murdoch made available to Robert the witty, complex poems of Alexander Pope, who became the young Burns's favourite poet. In summer 1773, William sent fourteen-year-old Robert for further study with Murdoch in Ayr. Robert learned some French, and Murdoch remembered him as a reader of newspapers. Studying with Murdoch also aroused Burns's teenage enthusiasm for sentimental novels like Henry Mackenzie's *The Man of Feeling* (1771), another taste that stayed with him all his life. Spurred on by Murdoch, Burns became a voracious reader of poetry, philosophy, fiction, newspapers and other texts. This was the poet who was soon reading enthusiastically a major work of philosophy, Adam Smith's *Theory of Moral Sentiments*, published in the year of Burns's birth. Burns never went to university. Yet, schooled in Scots song and folktale as well as in English language textual culture, he would develop as a poet who was thoroughly bicultural.

HIS FATHER'S INFLUENCE

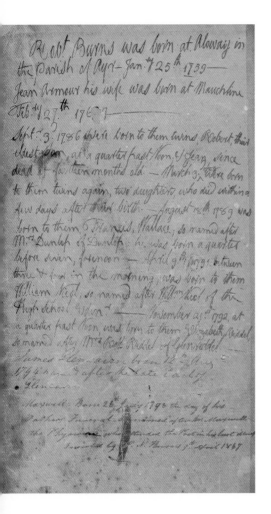

Above: page from Robert's family Bible. As well as his own name and birth date, he has inscribed those of Jean and their children. The name of the last born – Maxwell – was not written by the poet, as on the day he was born his father was being buried in Dumfries

Opposite, top left: the family Bible of William Burnes, showing the page with a register of the family, including the birth date of Robert. In later years, the poet himself was to write the date of his father's death on the same page

The seeds of inspiration sown in the young Robert's mind during his childhood – religious teachings, traditional Scottish songs, Betty Davidson's captivating stories – would all bear fruit in **The Cotter's Saturday Night**. Composed over the winter of 1785, the poem was largely inspired by Robert's own upbringing in Alloway and at the farms of Mount Oliphant and Lochlea.

Robert first recited the poem to his brother Gilbert while out walking one Sunday. Gilbert found the poem powerful and moving, recalling:

' ... the cotter in the Saturday night is an exact copy of my father in his manners, his family-devotion, and exhortations ... '

The poem describes the cotter, a peasant farmer with a tied cottage, returning home to his family at the end of his week's work. His wife and children wait to welcome him, 'expectant wee-things', just as Robert must have waited at the door to greet his own father. They enjoy a supper of 'healsome Porritch', before gathering around the fire in family worship.

The depiction of the cotter conducting family worship was a powerfully emotive image in the 1780s, and the poem not only established Burns's reputation in his own lifetime, but has endured as one of his most popular works. Many genre painters of the early nineteenth century were fascinated by Burns's descriptions of rural life.

The poem is also significant for Burns's take on the dignity of labour: the poor are neither patronised nor despised, but presented as noble and civilised. As testament to his own father who worked hard to ensure his children's education, Burns paints a picture of people who are articulate, dignified and at ease with themselves. They may be poor and have little prospect of material improvement, but they are educated in the things that matter. Through his words Burns succeeded in simultaneously engaging the landowning classes and empowering the working poor.

**From Scenes like these, old Scotia's grandeur springs,
That makes her lov'd at home, rever'd abroad:
Princes and lords are but the breath of kings,
'An honest man's the noblest work of God:'**

THE COTTER'S SATURDAY NIGHT (1785)

The chearfu' Supper done, wi' serious face,
They, round the *ingle*, form a circle wide;
The Sire turns o'er, with patriarchal grace,
The big *ha'-Bible*, ance his Father's pride:
His bonnet rev'rently is laid aside,
His *lyart haffets* wearing thin and bare;
Those strains that once did sweet in Zion glide,
He *wales* a portion with judicious care;
'And let us worship God!' he says with solemn air.

THE COTTER'S SATURDAY NIGHT (1785)

fireplace

*great Bible that lay in the
hall in mansion houses
grey sideburns*

chooses

19

A LIFE TIED TO THE LAND

By 1764, with the birth of Agnes and William's fourth child, conditions at the cottage in Alloway were becoming increasingly cramped. Robert was also approaching the age when he would be hired out as a day labourer to a neighbouring farmer, a course of action which his father sought to avoid at all costs. In an effort to secure his growing family's future, in 1766 William moved the family to the farm at Mount Oliphant, a couple of miles away.

Becoming a tenant farmer on the nominally 'improved' Mount Oliphant Farm was a step up in social rank. But Mount Oliphant, with its poor soil, would prove to be a desperate grind for the Burnes family, who teetered on the edge of financial disaster for the eleven years that they farmed there. As small land holdings were consolidated into larger, more productive and efficient units, an entire class of subsistence farmers in the Lowlands was gradually displaced or caught in a constant slog of effecting change from the old to the new, with little reward.

The strain of running the farm at Mount Oliphant with few resources, little money and minimal return aged Robert's father prematurely. To add to the family's troubles, their landlord died in November 1769. The estate passed into the control of a factor, who took a sterner line over delays in rent.

Burns described this period in a letter to Dr John Moore on 2 August 1787:

'My father's generous Master died; the farm proved a ruinous bargain; and, to clench the curse, we fell into the hands of a Factor who sat for the picture I have drawn of one in my Tale of two dogs ... We lived very poorly ... A Novel-Writer might perhaps have viewed these scenes with some satisfaction, but so did not I: my indignation yet boils at the recollection of the scoundrel tyrant's insolent, threatening epistles, which used to set us all in tears.'

Burns's experiences of tenant farming could not have been more significant for his writing. The fact that his poetry is firmly anchored in the realities of his time gives it a rich human meaning.

LOVE AND POESY

William Burnes could have had little idea of how his investment in his family's education would pay off. Although Robert's natural intuition and love of language had been apparent from a young age, it was while he was working on his father's farm aged fourteen that he penned his first song.

'The Poetic Genius of my Country found me as the prophetic bard Elijah did Elisha – at the plough; and threw her inspiring mantle over me. She bade me sing the loves, the joys, the rural scenes and rural pleasures of my natal Soil, in my native tongue: I tuned my wild, artless notes, as she inspired.'

(Dedication 'To the Noblemen and Gentlemen of the Caledonian Hunt', the preface to the Edinburgh edition of *Poems, Chiefly in the Scottish Dialect*, 1787)

The social aspect of rural living was hugely influential for Burns's poetry, for the Ayrshire of his youth was one of communal activity. Harvesting, herding, handling livestock, gathering fuel and building houses: all involved neighbours coming together to share tasks. As in all rural communities, the seasons dictated the year's activities. Harvest-time was without a doubt the most exciting, if demanding, time. It also offered the greatest opportunities for courtship:

'You know our country custom of coupling a man and woman together as Partners in the labors of Harvest. In my fifteenth autumn, my Partner was a bewitching creature who ... initiated me in a certain delicious Passion ... Thus with me began Love and Poesy ...'

(Letter from Robert Burns to Dr John Moore, 2 August 1787)

Background painting: Burns Monument by Patrick C Auld, 1839

Burns entitled his first song, **O once I lov'd a bonie lass** and names his muse as 'handsome Nell', or Helen Kilpatrick, the daughter of a local miller. Although the song will never rank amongst his best works, Burns felt warmly towards it, later writing:

' ... the first of my performances and done at an early period in my life, when my heart glowed with honest warm simplicity; unacquainted, and uncorrupted with the ways of a wicked world. The performance is, indeed, very puerile and silly: but I am always pleased with it, as it recalls to my mind those happy days when my heart was yet honest and my tongue was sincere.'

(Robert Burns, First Commonplace Book, 1783)

The landscape of his youth was pertinent to Burns not only for the romantic encounters it provided, but for the inspiration it offered for many of his works. As Burns's poetry developed to express great ideas, his physical imagery remained firmly rooted in the landscape around Alloway – songs such as **The Banks o' Doon** capture the countryside of his birth.

Top: Burns's writing set, comprising an ink bottle in a leather case, two quills and a knife, which he carried on his travels through the countryside

Above: full-length portrait of Robert Burns by Alexander Nasmyth (1758–1840). Nasmyth initially produced a pencil sketch of the poet standing deep in thought while on a visit with him to Roslin, near Edinburgh, although this was painted long after Burns's death (Scottish National Portrait Gallery)

Left: Robert Burns by Alexander Nasmyth, 1787 (Scottish National Portrait Gallery)

TAM O' SHANTER

Over two decades after Burns left Alloway, the memories of familiar places and the tales he heard in childhood were still very present in his mind. Burns's inspiration from Alloway would culminate in one of his greatest works – **Tam o' Shanter**.

Burns wrote and edited this epic narrative poem over the course of a year, finishing it in 1790. The previous year Burns had met the antiquarian and author Captain Francis Grose, who was planning to publish the second volume of his *Antiquities of Scotland*. A firm friendship soon grew up between the two and Burns suggested that Grose include Alloway Auld Kirk in his publication. Grose agreed on the condition that Burns supplied a tale of witchcraft to accompany the engraving of the ruined church. In June 1790 Burns wrote to Grose with three stories of witches, all centred on the ruined kirk at Alloway; from these came the story that would take shape in **Tam o' Shanter**.

This version of *Tam o' Shanter* is taken from an original manuscript written by Burns, which is in the museum collection.

Tam o' Shanter – A Tale

Aloway-kirk, the scene of the following Poem, is an old Ruin in Ayr-shire, hard by the great road from Ayr to Maybole, on the banks of the river, Doon, & near the old bridge of that name. A Drawing of this Ruin will make its appearance in Grose's antiquities of Scotland.

When *chapmen billies* **leave the street,**	*pedlars*
And *drouthy neebors* **neebors meet,**	*thirsty neighbours*
As market-days are wearing late,	
And folk begin to *tak the gate*;	*journey home*
While we sit bowsing at the *nappy,*	*ale*
And getting *fou,* **& unco happy,**	*drunk; uncommon(ly)*
We think na on the lang Scots miles,	
The mosses, waters, *slaps* **& styles,**	*bogs, pools*
That lie between us & our hame,	
Where sits our sulky, sullen dame,	
Gathering her brows like gathering storm,	
Nursing her wrath to keep it warm.	
This truth *fand* **honest Tam o' Shanter,**	*found*
As he frae Ayr *ae* **night did canter,**	*one*
(Auld Ayr wham ne'er a town surpasses	
For honest men & bonie lasses.)	
O Tam! hadst thou but been sae wise	
As taen thy ain wife Kate's advice!	
She tauld thee weel thou was a *skellum,*	*scoundrel / good for nothing*
A bletherin, blusterin, drunken *blellum*;	*babbler*
That, frae November till October,	
Ae market-day thou was na sober;	
That *ilka melder,* **wi' the Miller,**	*every last milling*
Thou sat as lang as thou had *siller*;	*money*
That every *naig* **was ca'd a shoe on,**	*nag*
The Smith & thee gat roarin fou on;	
That at the L__d's house even on Sunday,	
Thou drank wi' Kirkton Jean till Monday.	
She prophesied that, late or soon,	
Thou wad be found deep-drown'd in Doon;	
Or catch'd wi' warlocks in the *mirk*	*dark*
By Aloway's auld haunted kirk.	

Ah, gentle Dames! it *gars me greet*,   *makes me weep*
To think how mony counsels sweet,
How mony lengthen'd, sage advices,
The husband frae the wife despises!

But to our Tale: ae Market-night,
Tam had got planted unco right,
Fast by an ingle bleezin finely,
Wi' *reamin swats* that drank divinely;   *foaming ales*
And at his elbow, Souter Johnie,
His ancient, trusty, drouthy crony;
Tam lo'ed him like a very brither,
They had been fou for weeks thegither.
The night drave on wi' sangs & clatter,
And ay the ale was growing better:
The Landlady & Tam grew gracious,
Wi' favors, secret, sweet & precious;
The Souter tauld his queerest stories;
The Landlord's laugh was ready chorus;
The storm without might *rair* & rustle,   *roar*
Tam did na mind the storm a whistle.
Care, mad to see a man sae happy,
E'en drown'd himsel among the nappy.
As bees flee hame wi' *lades* o' treasure,   *loads*
The minutes wing'd their way wi' pleasure.
Kings may be blest, but Tam was glorious;
O'er a' the ills o' life victorious!

But pleasures are like poppies spread,
You sieze the flower, its bloom is shed;
Or like the snow falls in the river,
A moment white – then melts for ever;
Or like the borealis race,
That flit ere you can point their place;
Or like the rainbow's lovely form
Evanishing amid the storm.
Nae man can tether Time or Tide,
The hour approaches Tam *maun* ride;   *must*
That hour o' night's black arch the key-stane,
That dreary hour he mounts his beast in,
And *sic* a night he taks the road in   *such*
As ne'er poor sinner was abroad in.

As bees biz out wi' angry *fyke*,   *fuss*
When plundering herds assail their *byke*;   *hive*
As open *Pussie's* mortal foes,   *hare's*
When, pop, she starts before their nose;
As eager rins the Market-croud
When, "Catch the thief!" resounds aloud;
So Maggie rins, the witches follow,
Wi' mony an *eldritch* shout & hollo.   *unearthly*

Ah, Tam! Ah, Tam! thou'll get thy *fairin*!   *reward*
In hell they'll roast thee like a herrin!
In vain thy Kate awaits thy comin!
Kate soon will be a woefu' woman!!!

Now, do thy speedy utmost, Meg,
And win the key-stane o' the brig;
There, at them thou thy tail may toss,
A running stream they dare na cross!
But ere the key-stane she could make,
The *fient* a tail she had to shake.   *fiend*
For Nannie, far before the rest,
Hard upon noble Maggie prest,
And flew at Tam wi' furious *ettle*,   *aim*
But little *wist* she Maggie's mettle;   *was*
Ae spring brought off her Master *hale*, *whole*
But left behind her ain gray tail:
The *Carline* claught her by the rump,   *witch*
And left poor Maggie scarce a stump.

Now wha this Tale o' truth shall read,
Each man & mother's son take heed:
Whene'er to Drink ye are inclin'd,
Or Cutty-sarks run in your mind,
Think, ye may buy the joys o'er dear;
Remember Tam o' Shanter's Meare!

The wind blew as 'twad blawn its last;
The rattling showers rose on the blast;
The speedy gleams the darkness swallow'd;
Loud, deep & lang, the thunder bellow'd:
That night, a child might understand
The deil had business on his hand.

Weel mounted on his gray meare, Meg,
A better never lifted leg,
Tam *skelpit* on thro' dub & mire,   strode
Despising wind, and rain, & fire;
Whyles holding fast his gude blue bonnet,   now
Whyles crooning o'er an auld Scots sonnet;
Whyles glowring round wi' prudent cares,   staring
Lest bogles catch him unawares;
Kirk-Aloway was drawing nigh,
Where ghaists & *houlets* nightly cry.   owls

By this time he was cross the ford,
Where in the snaw the chapman *smoor'd*;   smothered
And past the *birks* & *meikle* stane,   birches; big
Where drunken Charlie brak's neck-bane;
And thro' the *whins* & by the cairn,   gorse
Where hunters fand the murder'd bairn;
And near the thorn, *aboon* the well,   above
Where Mungo's mither hang'd hersel.
Before him Doon pours all his floods,
The doubling storm roars thro' the woods,
The lightenings flash from pole to pole,
Near & more near the thunders roll;
When, glimmering thro' the groaning trees,
Kirk-Aloway seem'd in a *bleeze*;   blaze
Thro' *ilka* bore the beams were glancing,   every chink
And loud resounded mirth & dancing.

Inspiring, bold *John Barleycorn*,   alcohol, beer
What dangers thou canst make us scorn!
Wi' *tippeny* we fear nae evil,   twopenny ale
Wi' *usquabae* we'll face the devil.   whisky
The swats sae ream'd in Tammie's *noddle*, brain
Fair play, he car'd na deils a *boddle*;   farthing
But Maggie stood, right sair astonish'd,
Till by the heel & hand admonish'd,
She ventur'd forward on the light,
And, wow! Tam saw an unco sight!

Warlocks & witches in a dance,
Nae *cotillon* brent new frae France,   *dance*
But hornpipes, jigs, strathspeys & reels,
Put life & *mettle* in their heels.   *spirit*
A *winnock-bunker* in the east,   *window seat*
There sat auld Nick in shape o' beast,
A *towzie tyke*, black, grim & large,   *shaggy dog*
To gie them music was his charge:
He screw'd the pipes & *gart them skirl*,   *made them squeal*
Till roof & rafters a' did *dirl*.   *ring*
Coffins stood round, like open *presses*,   *cupboards*
That shaw'd the Dead in their last dresses,
And (by some devilish *cantraip slight*)   *magic device*
Each in its cauld hand held a light.
By which heroic Tam was able
To note upon the haly table,
A murderer's banes in gibbet-*airns*;   *irons*
Twa *span-lang*, wee, unchirsten'd bairns;   *hand-length*
A thief new-cutted frae a *rape*,   *rope*
Wi' his last gasp his *gab* did gape;   *mouth*
Five tomahawks wi' blude red-rusted;
Five scymitars wi' murder crusted;
A garter that a babe had strangled;
A knife a father's throat had mangled,
Whom his ain son of life bereft,
The gray hairs yet stack to the heft:
With mair o' horrible & awefu',
Which even to name wad be unlawfu'.
Three Lawyer's tongues, turn'd inside out,
Wi' lies seam'd like a beggar's *clout*;   *cloth*
Three Priest's hearts, rotten, black as muck,
Lay stinking, vile, in every *neuk*.   *corner*

As Tammie glowr'd, amaz'd & curious,
The mirth & fun grew fast & furious:
The Piper loud & louder blew,
The Dancers quick and quicker flew;
They reel'd, they set, they crost, they *cleekit*,   *linked arms*
Till ilka Carlin *swat & reekit*,   *sweat; stank*
And *coost* her *duddies* on the *wark*,   *cast; ragged clothes; floor*
And *linket* at it in her *sark*.   *danced around; underskirt*

Now Tam! O Tam! had thae been *queans*   *young girls*
A' plump & strappin in their teens,
Their sarks, instead o' *creeshie flainen,*   *greasy flannel*
Been snaw-white, seventeen-hunder linen;
Thir breeks o' mine, my only pair,
That *ance* were *plush* o' gude blue hair,   *once; silken fabric*
I wad hae gien them off my *hurdies*   *buttocks*
For ae blink o' the bonie *burdies!*   *maidens*

But wither'd *beldams,* auld & droll,   *old women*
Rigwoodie **hags wad** *spean* a foal,   *gnarled; suckle*
Loupin & flingin on a *crummock,*   *stick*
I wonder did na turn thy stomach.

But Tam *kend* what was what *fu' brawlie;*   *knew; very well*
There was ae winsome wench & *walie,*   *jolly*
That night enlisted in the core,
(Lang after, kend on Carrick-shore;
For mony a beast to dead she shot,
And perish'd mony a bonie boat,
And shook baith meikle corn & *bear,*   *barley*
And kept the country-side in fear:)
Her *cutty-sark* o' Paisley *harn,*   *short shirt / undergarment; coarse cloth*
That while a lassie she had worn,
In longitude tho' sorely scanty,
It was her best, & she was *vaunty.*   *proud*
Ah, little thought thy reverend graunie,
That sark she *coft* for her wee Nannie   *bought*
Wi' twa pund Scots ('twas a' her riches)
Should ever grac'd a dance o' witches!

But here my Muse her wing maun *cour,*   *droop*
Sic flights are far beyond her power,
To sing, how Nannie *lap* and *flang,*   *leaped and kicked*
(A *souple jad* she was & strang)   *supple lass*
And how Tam stood like ane bewitch'd,
And thought his very *een* enrich'd;   *eyes*
Even Satan glowr'd, & *fidg'd fu' fain,*   *moved excitedly*
And *hotch'd,* & blew wi' might & main: *jerked*
Till first ae *caper* – *syne* anither –   *dance; then*
Tam *tint* his reason a' thegither,   *lost*
And roars out – "Weel done, Cutty-sark!"
And in an instant all was dark;
And scarcely had he Maggie rallied,
When out the hellish legion sallied.

Widely regarded as Burns's masterpiece, **Tam o' Shanter** embodies the best of Burns – his wit, wisdom, humour, humanity and his searing observation of character. Burns himself was pleased with the work, writing that it 'shew in my opinion ... a finishing polish that I despair of ever excelling'. Written in a mixture of Burns's Ayrshire dialect and English, the poem is centred on the character of Tam, who was modelled on the real-life person of Douglas Graham, a tenant of the farm of Shanter on Carrick shore. Graham is said to have owned a boat called the *Tam o' Shanter*. His wife Helen, infamous for her sharp tongue, also features in the tale as the shrewish Kate, who sits at home and awaits the arrival of her drunken husband:

> **Gathering her brows like gathering storm,**
> **Nursing her wrath to keep it warm.**

Early on in the poem, Burns locates the scene: 'This truth fand honest Tam o' Shanter, As he frae Ayr ae night did canter'. Like Tam, 'Weel mounted on his gray meare, Meg', the poem gallops along as Tam, the worse for drink, rides through the Ayrshire countryside. But the main events of the poem take place when Tam reaches Alloway Auld Kirk, the ruined church which had inhabited the imagination of Burns since his childhood, with its associated tales of the Devil and the supernatural. Suddenly, 'Tam saw an unco sight!' The sight is Alloway Kirk, ablaze with light and resounding to the sound of 'hornpipes, jigs, strathspeys & reels' as witches and warlocks dance faster and faster accompanied by the Devil on his bagpipes. A drunken Tam watches silently as the dancing witches begin to cast off their clothes. But eventually, beguiled by one witch called Nannie whose 'cutty-sark' or undershirt is too small for her, Tam forgets himself,

> **And roars out – "Weel done, Cutty-sark!"**
> **And in an instant all was dark;**

The witches round on Tam and there follows a fast and furious chase as Tam frantically spurs his horse on to cross the Brig o' Doon, for superstition states that witches cannot cross running water. Meg and Tam only just make it, as Nannie, first among the 'hellish legion' chasing them, grabs the horse's tail,

> **The Carline claught her by the rump,**
> **And left poor Maggie scarce a stump.**

Burns concludes with the tongue-in-cheek lines on the perils of drunkenness and lechery:

> **Whene'er to Drink ye are inclin'd,**
> **Or Cutty-sarks run in your mind,**
> **Think, ye may buy the joys o'er dear;**
> **Remember Tam o' Shanter's Meare!**

Five engravings of scenes from Tam o' Shanter *by John Faed, c1855*

THE ALLOWAY EFFECT

BRIG O' DOON

Brig o' Doon is a single-span stone bridge dating probably from the fifteenth century. Robert would have known this bridge well as a child – it was the main crossing over the river at the time and his father would have used it every day on his way to and from work.

A new bridge was built downstream in 1816, but the Brig o' Doon has twice escaped demolition due to its links to Burns's poem, *Tam o' Shanter*.

Tourists sometimes believe that the Brig o' Doon is the site of Brigadoon, the mythical village that only appears for a day every century, as portrayed in the 1954 film of the same name. In fact, there is no connection except in name.

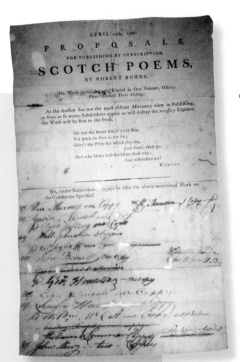

THE KILMARNOCK EDITION

At the beginning of 1786, Robert turned 27. His life seemed to be lurching from one crisis to another. His first child had recently been born out of wedlock to Elizabeth Paton, a servant girl working at Lochlea Farm. In the summer of 1786, Robert contracted a 'form of wedlock' with Mauchline lass Jean Armour. In the autumn of 1786 Jean gave birth to twins fathered by Robert. Jean's parents were furious and dispatched their daughter to stay with relatives in Paisley. In July, Jean's father, James Armour, had issued a writ for Robert's arrest to recover substantial damages on his daughter's behalf. Robert's correspondence at the time gives an idea of his misery.

This sheet, dated 14 April 1786, is thought to be the only copy to survive of the proposal to print 'Scotch Poems' by Robert Burns

'Would you believe it? Armour has got a warrant to throw me in jail till I find security for an enormous sum ... and I am wandering from one friend's house to another, and like a true son of the Gospel "have no where to lay my head." ... I write it in a moment of rage, reflecting on my miserable situation – exiled, abandoned, forlorn ...'

(Letter from Robert Burns to John Richmond, 30 July 1786)

Opposite, top: Burns in an Edinburgh Drawing Room, unknown artist, mid-nineteenth century. Dressed in his riding boots, Burns was christened the 'ploughman poet' and was treated as something of a novelty in polite Edinburgh society

Right: the 'Kilmarnock edition' of Poems was printed at Ayrshire's only printing press in the summer of 1786 and sold out within a few weeks. This copy is one of only 65 known to exist, and is arguably one of Scotland's most important publications

His complicated personal life, lack of money and a life tied to the land held increasingly less appeal. In an attempt to escape his situation, he contemplated leaving Scotland to take up a new life overseeing slaves on a sugar plantation in Jamaica. But with little money, Burns needed to raise funds for his passage and the idea of publishing his works came to the fore.

'Before leaving my native country for ever, I resolved to publish my Poems ... I was pretty sure my Poems would meet with some applause; but at the worst, the roar of the Atlantic would deafen the voice of Censure ...'

(Letter from Robert Burns to Dr John Moore, 2 August 1787)

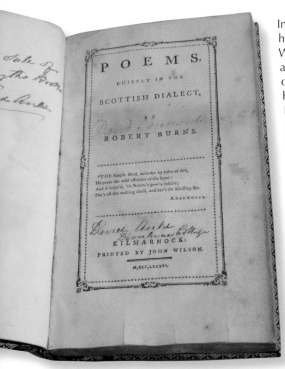

In the event, Burns changed his plans to emigrate and focused all his energy on publishing his work. He approached the printer John Wilson, based in Kilmarnock. Wilson was cautious about the venture and in an attempt to reduce the financial risk he requested that Burns obtain a list of potential purchasers. This Burns duly did, circulating his 'Proposals for Publishing by Subscription Scotch Poems, by Robert Burns'. Priced at three shillings a copy, the cost represented the equivalent of around a week's income for an average worker, but despite this Burns received over 350 promises to buy his book. On 31 July 1786, 612 copies of *Poems, Chiefly in the Scottish Dialect* were published to rapturous acclaim. The book, which contains some of his best writing, including *The Twa Dogs*, *Address to the Deil*, *Halloween*, *The Cotter's Saturday Night*, *To a Mouse* and *To a Mountain-Daisy*, was an immediate success, selling out within a month. Burns found himself catapulted into the limelight and the course of his life changed forever.

In the autumn Burns headed to Edinburgh to arrange the publication of a second edition of his *Poems*. He became a big hit with the literati and, in December, Henry Mackenzie, one of Burns's favourite authors, praised the 'power of genius' of 'this Heaven-taught ploughman' in an influential essay published in the magazine *The Lounger*. The 'Edinburgh edition' of *Poems* appeared in April 1787, which succeeded in establishing Burns's reputation throughout Britain and beyond – before long, versions were printed in London, Dublin, Belfast, Philadelphia and New York. Burns sold the copyright of his work for one hundred guineas, but in doing so signed away his rights to any future financial benefit.

BURNS IN LOVE

Love and poetry went together for Burns. Indeed, the most prolific period in Burns's creative life also coincided with one of the most tangled periods in his love life. In the two years from April 1785 to April 1787, Burns took three lovers, fathered three children, attempted to emigrate to Jamaica with one partner whilst unofficially married to another … and published two volumes of poems.

Margaret Campbell ('Highland Mary')

Shortly before he published his first volume of poems Burns, estranged from Jean Armour, who was then unmarried and pregnant, began an affair with Margaret Campbell, later mythologised as 'Highland Mary'.

'Highland Mary' was one of Burns's most celebrated loves. He first met Margaret when she worked as a nursemaid for Burns's lawyer friend, Gavin Hamilton in Mauchline; by spring 1786 they were probably lovers. It is certainly possible that he planned for Margaret to emigrate with him to Jamaica, but her early death in September 1786 prevented any plans he may have had from coming to fruition.

In the 1920s, 130 years after her death, Margaret's grave in Greenock was exhumed and moved to another location in the town to accommodate an expanding shipyard. An infant's coffin was found next to her remains, giving rise to speculation that Burns's lover may have died giving birth to his child.

The compelling combination of tragedy and love saw 'Highland Mary' eulogised a generation after her death. Her story was romanticised in both print and paint. Publications such as *Memoirs of Women Loved and Celebrated by Poets* (by Mrs Jameson, 1837) and paintings such as *The Betrothal of Burns and Highland Mary* by William Henry Midwood in the 1860s presented an overly romanticised and sentimental view of the couple.

Jean Armour

'Our Robbie should have had twa wives.' **(Attributed to Jean Armour)**

Robert Burns first met Jean Armour in 1785 and they were officially married three years later, by which time Jean had already given birth to four of their nine children – two sets of twins. Although Burns could not be said to be a faithful husband, fathering at least four illegitimate children, he did love Jean and she directly inspired over a dozen of his songs.

Burns wrote of his wife:

'… I have got the handsomest figure, the sweetest temper, the soundest constitution, and the kindest heart in the county.'

(Letter from Robert Burns to Margaret Chalmers, 16 September 1788)

Jean, in turn, stood by him, taking on the care and upbringing of her husband's illegitimate offspring on more than one occasion.

There are no early portraits of Jean and this engraving shows her when she was a widow, by G Cook after John Alexander Gilfillan, 1826

Agnes McLehose ('Clarinda')

**But to see her, was to love her;
Love but her, and love for ever.**

Ae fond kiss (1791)

When Burns went to Edinburgh to publish the second edition of his *Poems*, he made some influential lifelong friendships and embarked on a relationship with Mrs Agnes 'Nancy' McLehose. Burns became infatuated with Agnes, his social superior, and the couple began a passionate correspondence where they masked their identities using the classical pen names of Clarinda and Sylvander. Burns's relationship with Clarinda was literary rather than physical, but he seemed to be deeply in love with her and wrote one of his best love songs, *Ae fond kiss*, for her on their parting in 1791:

**Ae fond kiss, and then we sever;
Ae fareweel, and then for ever!**

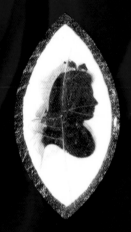

Silhouette of Clarinda by John Miers, 1788. Robert asked Agnes McLehose to pose for this tiny portrait 'for a breast pin to wear next my heart'

Far left: Bible containing a lock of 'Highland Mary's' hair, with an inscription suggesting that Robert was making a solemn oath to her

Left: romantic depiction of Burns and 'Highland Mary' by Hamilton

BURNS AGAINST THE ESTABLISHMENT

Burns was an innovator. He thought differently, did not conform to his 'place' in society and often expressed ideas that caught people off balance. In 1781, at the age of 22, Burns was initiated into the Freemasons at St David's Lodge in Tarbolton. Associated with ideas of brotherhood that overstepped boundaries of rank and nation, Freemasonry would prove to be an influential force throughout Burns's life. Not only did it offer him an outlet and system of belief, but also a network of friends and connections helpful in furthering his career.

However, free thinking frequently brought Burns into conflict with the establishment. In 1785 he wrote **The Holy Fair**. This poem is based on the Mauchline Holy Fair, a twice-yearly event that attracted large numbers of people to hear outdoor preachings prior to taking communion; it was also one of the biggest social occasions.

Burns used the poem to expose the hypocrisy and double-standards he saw in the preaching of Kirk ministers, producing a scathing attack against those in power who he felt abused their authority. In the poem, the narrator accompanies three girls – allegories of Fun, Hypocrisy and Superstition – on their way to Mauchline Holy Fair.

This Masonic apron was presented to Burns in December 1791. He wore it during meetings of Lodge St Andrew No. 179 in Dumfries

'I'm *gaun* to Mauchline holy fair,	*going*
'To spend an hour in *daffin*;	*larking, having fun*
'*Gin* ye'll go there, *yon runkl'd* pair,	*If; yonder wrinkled [the 'pair'*
'We will get famous laughin	*are Hypocrisy and Superstition]*
At them this day.'	

Burns's satire exposes the moral tug-of-war that those attending the Holy Fair found themselves in, torn between the teachings of the Kirk and the more earthly pleasures of drinking and 'houghmagandie' (fornication).

But it was not only the hypocritical teachings of the Kirk with which Burns took issue. Very early in his life he was acutely aware of the social distinctions which divided his class from the wealthy landowners and merchants, although this did not stop him from forming strong and lasting friendships with members of the gentry. In his introduction to The Commonplace Book Burns wrote of himself: 'As he was but little indebted to scholastic education, and bred at a plough-tail, his performances must be strongly tinctured with his unpolished, rustic way of life.' Yet it was precisely this life of demanding physical work and poverty, combined with his sharp awareness of social disadvantage, that drove Burns to find an expressive creative outlet. He began to write poetry as 'some kind of counterpoise' to his adverse circumstances.

Too lowly to be granted a vote, Burns used his writing desk as his ballot box and his pen to make his voice heard. Burns grew up at a time when the Radical movement was seeking political reform, and became a natural sympathiser with its aims. In his most famous democratic political song, he dares to speak up for the common man, attacks social rank, and proclaims the coming of a new age of universal brotherhood.

Is there, for honest Poverty
That hings his head, and a' that;
The coward-slave, we pass him by,
We dare be poor for a' that!

A MAN'S A MAN FOR A' THAT (1795)

RADICAL REFORM

Scotland was very much aware of war in the late eighteenth century as first the American War of Independence (1775–83) and then the French Revolution of 1789 and the subsequent wars with France hit the headlines. Newspaper circulation boomed as the public, with a growing interest in international events, followed the wars' progress. And, as the French embraced an enlightened constitution, Radicals in Scotland began to demand the same. The Revolution demonstrated that ordinary people could participate in the governance of their country, that they could change the status quo and that they could shape constitutions to reflect their views. It was these ideas which appealed to Burns.

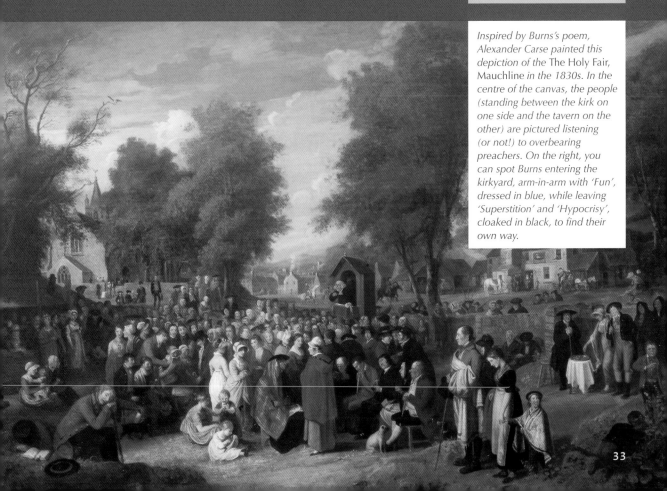

Inspired by Burns's poem, Alexander Carse painted this depiction of the The Holy Fair, Mauchline *in the 1830s. In the centre of the canvas, the people (standing between the kirk on one side and the tavern on the other) are pictured listening (or not!) to overbearing preachers. On the right, you can spot Burns entering the kirkyard, arm-in-arm with 'Fun', dressed in blue, while leaving 'Superstition' and 'Hypocrisy', cloaked in black, to find their own way.*

Songs and songwriting

(Letter from Robert Burns to James Hoy, 6 November 1787)

The seeds for what would prove to become Burns's chief passion for the rest
of his life were sown during his first visits to Edinburgh in 1786–7. There he
met a kindred spirit in James Johnson, an engraver specialising in printing and
selling music who was about to publish the first volume of his **Scots Musical
Museum**, a collection of 100 traditional Scottish songs.

Inspired by this new-found interest, Burns set off on a series of journeys
through Scotland, first to the Borders and then north to Stirlingshire and
ending in the Highlands. On his travels he collected songs and tunes, many
of which would later make an appearance in further volumes of **The Scots
Musical Museum**:

'I have been absolutely crazed about it, collecting old stanzas, and
every information remaining respecting their origin, authors, &c., &c.'

(Letter from Robert Burns to Rev John Skinner, 25 October 1787)

Love of music and song had been instilled in Burns from his earliest days
cradled in his mother's arms in the cottage at Alloway. Drawing on these
first experiences, Burns threw his energies into collecting, writing and re-
modelling Scottish songs. He sent James Johnson around 200 songs and
ultimately became the main driving force behind the next four volumes.
Burns refused to accept any fee: this was the work of a man who felt
passionately for his country and its rich cultural heritage.

His work on **The Scots Musical Museum** soon earned him the unrivalled
position as the national authority on Scottish songs. In 1792, George
Thomson, another collector of songs, wrote to Burns telling of his plan to
bring out a volume of 'the most favourite of our national melodies' and
appealed to Burns to write 'twenty or twenty-five songs' for the collection. In
the event, Burns wrote over 160 songs for Thomson's **A Select Collection of
Original Scotish Airs for the Voice**, again without a fee.

The first of five volumes of this work was published in 1793. Burns
continued to send Thomson song after song, although by 1794 his health
was becoming a cause for concern. Despite this, Burns dedicated much
of the last years of his life to collecting and editing traditional songs
from around Scotland. In doing so he made a major contribution to our
knowledge and understanding of the genre, for before then traditional music
was rarely written down.

'... let our National Music preserve its native features. They are, I
own, frequently wild, & unreduceable to the modern rules; but on
that very eccentricity, perhaps, depends a great part of their effect.'

(Letter from Robert Burns to George Thomson, 26 April 1793)

And surely ye'll be your pint-stoup,
And surely I'll be mine;
And we'll tak a cup o' kindness yet,
For auld lang syne. —

We twa hae run about the braes,
And pou't the gowans fine;
But we've wandered mony a weary fitt
Sin auld lang syne.

We twa hae paidl't in the burn
Frae morning sun till dine;
But seas between us braid hae roar'd
Sin auld lang syne. —

Auld lang syne

'... the old song of the olden times, & which has never been in print, nor even in manuscript, untill I took it down from an old man's singing; is enough to recommend any air'

(Letter from Robert Burns to George Thomson, September 1793)

Auld lang syne was an example of Burns's reworking, rewriting and adding to an old ballad which he came across during his travels. He liked the Scots phrase 'auld lang syne', meaning 'for old time's sake' which he thought 'exceedingly expressive'.

Top: fragment of Auld lang syne, *written in Burns's hand, 1788*

Above: The Scots Musical Museum, with Burns's improved version of Auld lang syne

my pleasures. — I have lately drank deep
of the cup of affliction. — The Autumn robbe[d]
me of my only daughter & darling child, & that
at a distance too & so rapidly as to put it out o[f]
my power to pay the last duties to her — I ha[ve]
scarcely began to recover from that shock, when [I]
became myself the victim of a most severe
Rheumatic fever, & long the die spun doubtf[ul]
until after many weeks of a sick-bed it seems t[o]
have turned up more life, & I am beginning
to crawl across my room, & once indeed have be[en]
my own door in the street. —

When Pleasure fascinates the mental sight,
  Affliction purifies the visual ray;
Religion hails the drear, the untried night,
  That shuts, for ever shuts! Life's doubtful day[.]

ILL HEALTH AND DEATH

By 1795 Burns's health had deteriorated badly. The death of his daughter Elizabeth in September appeared to deepen his depression and during the winter he became increasingly unwell. His illness may have had its roots in his youth. Burns's brother Gilbert wrote:

'My brother, at the age of thirteen, assisted in threshing the crop of corn, and at fifteen was the principal labourer on the farm, for we had no hired servants male or female. I doubt not, but the hard labour and sorrow of this period of his life, was in a great measure, the cause of that depression of spirits with which Robert was so often afflicted through his whole life afterwards.'

As his health worsened, Burns was sent by his doctor to Brow, where, in an attempt to relieve his symptoms, he immersed himself in the freezing waters of the Solway Firth. Only a few weeks later, on 21 July 1796, the 'Heaven-taught ploughman' turned 'Caledonia's Bard' died at the age of 37. He was buried in the graveyard of St Michael's Church in Dumfries with full military honours.

Experts now think that Burns died from heart disease, probably endocarditis (an inflammation of the lining of the heart). This is a known complication of rheumatic fever, which Burns may have contracted as a teenager while working in the fields. But during the last year of his life Burns also suffered terribly with toothache, and the endocarditis may have been the result of a dental abscess flooding his bloodstream with bacteria.

THE MYTHS

Over the years, people have blamed Burns's early death on numerous causes – including alcohol, sexually transmitted disease, lead poisoning, mercury poisoning and tuberculosis. Recent medical research has disproved these theories. Some conspiracy theorists have even blamed the death of Burns on the government on the grounds of his Radicalism, but this remains speculative and unproven.

Above: Robert Burns by Alexander Reid, 1795–6. This portrait was painted during the last eighteen months of Burns's life, and the poet considered it to be the best likeness of him (Scottish National Portrait Gallery)

Left: pair of duelling pistols which belonged to Burns and were given to his physician, Dr William Maxwell, while Burns was on his deathbed. Burns's youngest son, born on the day of his funeral, was named after Dr Maxwell

Opposite: Burns suffered from bouts of ill health throughout his life. In this letter to his friend Mrs Dunlop, he complains of a severe rheumatic fever from which he is only beginning to recover. Six months later he was dead

LEGACY OF BURNS

PERFORMING BURNS

EDDI READER, SINGER AND SONGWRITER

This beautiful instrument was owned by Burns; it is a guittar, an early form of the modern guitar

The Robert Burns story became part of my story about nine years ago, when I was asked to sing *My love is like a red, red rose* on a TV production for Burns night. I knew only a handful of Robert Burns's songs at this time. Songs I had heard sung as a younger girl, when I used to frequent the folk clubs of Scotland looking for free entry with a floor spot. If they liked you then you might get a booking, or at least another floor spot.

Red red rose was something I had, of course, heard but I'd never imagined singing it. While learning that song, something important happened to me: I felt like I had been singing it all my life and it was an old friend come home to me. Shortly after that concert, in May the same year, I was invited to sing a few Robert Burns songs with the Royal Scottish National Orchestra during their Robert Burns celebration gig in the grounds of Culzean Castle, Ayrshire. I took the only Burns tunes I knew: *Green grow the rashes, O* and *Auld lang syne*, plus a new version of *My love is like a red, red rose*, and worked alongside Kevin McCrae, who arranged the strings of the RSNO around my acoustic versions of the Burns songs.

That evening, as the sun was setting over the still water and Ailsa Craig, I nestled into the beauty of the gardens. The hundreds of people who had come to celebrate Burns with us were getting a little drunk. Children and birds were late to their bed. As the first bars of the orchestration of *Green grow the rashes, O* began, I felt like Robert was with me as I sung directly to the three beautiful, giggling lassies shouting '**Gawn yursel Eddi!!**' from the side of the garden, near the bar and the roses.

As I floated through the strings and lilted with the crowd during the chorus, I had a feeling that I needed to immerse myself in this man's work. I felt a calling for it and somehow I felt I would find a friend in his writings and his story. I had been living away from Scotland for 23 years and decided there and then that I would pack myself and my two children up and move home.

I spent the rest of the spring and summer finding more of Robert's work to sing, which led to me discovering his life story – his passions, the journeys he took and the terrible tragedy of his early death in poverty. I wanted to record with an orchestra to give him the magnificence his words and tunes deserve and perhaps find non-classical musicians that would represent the musicians Robert himself would have played with in the bars of Ayrshire.

I felt a duty to indulge my own passion in him and, perhaps for the briefest moments, raise him from the dead. I wanted – and still want – to send him a message, to show him how loved and cherished his words and ideas have stayed.

I invite you to do the same.

Burns and the Scots Language

Matthew Fitt, Writer and Education Director at Itchy Coo

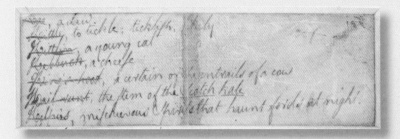

Left: all that remains of the glossary that Burns produced for the second edition of his Poems *to explain the Scots words*

Robert Burns had a way with words – and the majority of them were Scots words. He spoke in Scots, wrote in Scots and sang in it too. Scots was his mother tongue. It was the language in his head and heart and it was the medium in which he composed nearly all of his best poems and songs.

Lines like 'When drouthy neebors neebors meet', 'A daimen icker in a thrave' and 'Painch, tripe or thairm' can leave most modern readers pretty well stumped. The passions, hopes and fears of the society in which he lived were expressed almost exclusively in Scots. The idiom and vocabulary of those around him informed and shaped his genius as a writer. Arguably, the Scots language is what makes Burns Burns.

Yet in most modern celebrations of his life, the Scots language is unlikely to get even a passing mention. Many of those who give the Immortal Memory at a Burns Supper have forgotten how important the language was to Burns as a writer.

With the rising status of English after the Union of 1707, Scots lost its place as the official language of Scotland. Noticing how rapidly it was falling out of use, Burns made a conscious choice to write in his mother tongue. By doing so, he arrested its decline, legitimising the language as a vehicle for poetry and song. How many of us learned to recite a Scots poem in primary school?

Burns was fully aware of the other poets before him who had written great literature in Scots.

The medieval makars – William Dunbar, Robert Henryson and Sir David Lindsay – are part of a long literary tradition that was continued after Burns by Robert Louis Stevenson, Hugh MacDiarmid and Violet Jacob, and in our time by Edwin Morgan, Irvine Welsh and Liz Lochhead.

Scots is the official name of the West Germanic language spoken in modern Scotland. Recognised as a language in its own right by the Scottish and UK governments, it is protected within the EU by a European Charter. One-third of today's population speak a modern version of the same language used by Burns in the eighteenth century.

But a recent government survey revealed that most of us consider Scots to be 'slang'. How did we as a nation come to think so little of the language of our national poet? Unfortunately it is because we have not been the best custodians of this important part of our linguistic heritage. For far too long we have awarded our children prizes for reciting Scots each January 25th and then told them off for speaking it the rest of the year. However, those schools which value Scots as a normal part of learning throughout the year report substantial improvements in the attainment, behaviour and confidence of many of their pupils. Burns would have approved of this.

Aye, we should honour our national bard but we should also accept that the language which inspired Robert Burns has a positive role to play in modern Scottish life.

THE IMMORTAL MEMORY: BIRTH OF A LEGEND

MEMENTO MORI

The night before Jean Armour's funeral in 1834, the mausoleum where Burns's body was interred was opened. Phrenologists seized the opportunity to make a cast of Burns's skull. Then considered a science, phrenology was believed to identify personality traits by reading bumps and fissures in the skull. The subsequent report on Burns concluded that his skull was larger than average, that he was good with language and possessed skills in mathematics.

Only a year after Burns's death, *A Memoir of the Life of the Late Robert Burns* appeared in print. In it, the author Robert Heron asserted that the poet yielded 'readily to any temptation that offered', thus setting the myth in motion of Burns as a drunken womaniser. Three years later, a subsequent memoir of the poet's life was written by James Currie. The historian and writer Thomas Carlyle was later to denounce this work, saying of Currie, 'He everywhere introduces him with a certain patronising, apologetic air'. Currie, like many others after him, portrayed Burns as a flawed genius, a man whose weakness for drink had brought him to an early grave. It took Robert Chambers' *Life and Works of Robert Burns*, published in 1851, to redress the balance. Chambers' work helped to shake off the idea that Burns was simply a wonderful peasant, and instead asserted that he was one of the greatest poetical spirits; this was the first biography to recognise the universal appeal of the poet.

Plaudits also came from hugely respected men like John Ruskin, who declared: 'The books that have most influenced me are Coleridge and Keats in my youth, Burns as I grew older and wiser'.

Burns's fame grew to extraordinary proportions. The Victorians were fanatical in their adoration of Burns, collecting all sorts of souvenirs and mementos relating to him and his life. Wooden souvenirs made from trees grown on the banks of the Doon or the rafters of Alloway Auld Kirk were highly sought after by enthusiastic Victorian collectors.

a bit of wood broken from the Coffin of Robert Burns, when it was raised from the grave at the burial of his Widow - Presented ...

Tiny fragment of wood broken from Burns's coffin in 1834.

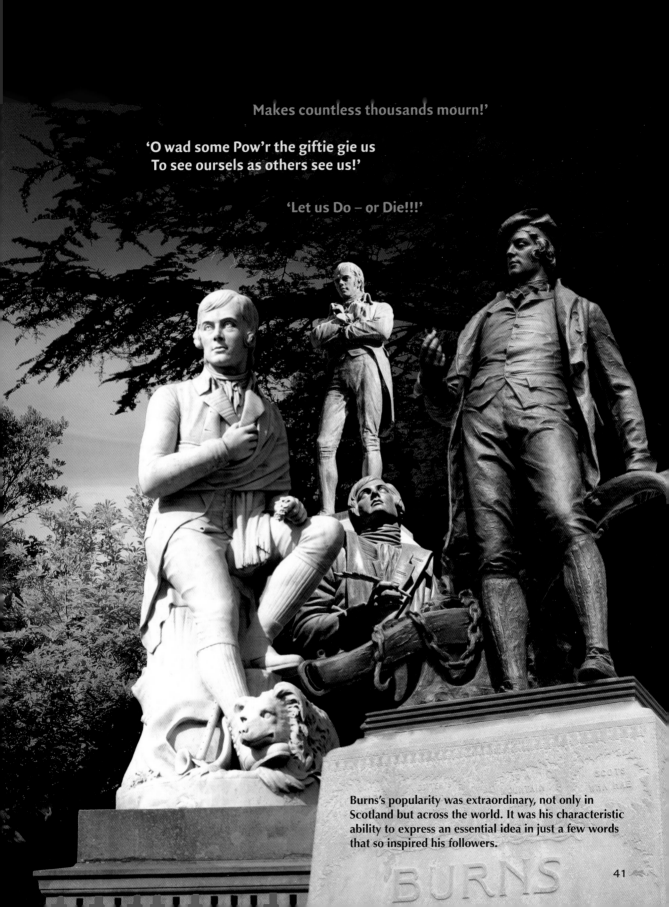

'Makes countless thousands mourn!'

'O wad some Pow'r the giftie gie us
To see oursels as others see us!'

'Let us Do – or Die!!!'

Burns's popularity was extraordinary, not only in
Scotland but across the world. It was his characteristic
ability to express an essential idea in just a few words
that so inspired his followers.

BURNS

VISITORS TO ALLOWAY

Above: painting by an unknown artist showing the 1844 Burns Festival procession, which started in Ayr, then passed over the old and new brigs o' Doon, before entering the festival site at Burns Monument. Burns's three surviving sons were guests of honour at the event, which attracted over 100,000 participants

By the start of the nineteenth century the cottage at Alloway had become an alehouse. In 1801 the first ever Burns Supper was held here when a small group of friends gathered to share a meal and raise a glass to the poet's memory. Soon, Burns Clubs started to spring up to celebrate the poet, many of which are still active today.

But for many the focus on Burns would always be his birthplace at Alloway, and it was here that the first visitors came to pay homage. One of those inspired to visit Burns's birthplace was the poet John Keats, who wrote of his visit in 1818: 'I had no conception that the native place of Burns was so beautiful.'

Since then there have been many more famous visitors to Burns Cottage, among them Alfred, Lord Tennyson, HRH the Queen and the Duke of Edinburgh, Muhammad Ali, Clark Gable and Vidal Sassoon.

Burns's literary influence is equally wide-ranging, from books such as *Of Mice and Men* by John Steinbeck to the lyrics of musicians like Bob Dylan, who has said that **My love is like a red, red rose** was his greatest inspiration.

BURNS MONUMENT TRUST AND BURNS MONUMENT

' ... a Monument to the Memory of the Ayrshire Bard, where he first drew breath, and in that County where his genius was fostered and Matured ... shall be erected at or near the Place of his Birth.'

(First minute of Burns Monument Trust, 24 March 1814)

A group of individuals in Alloway formed the Burns Monument Trust in 1814 to raise funds for a suitable memorial to Robert Burns. They succeeded in raising the cost of building the monument by subscriptions from Burns lovers throughout the world. In 1820 the foundation stone for Burns Monument was laid by Sir Alexander Boswell, son of diarist James Boswell and chairman of the Trust, and the finished monument opened to the public on 4 July 1823.

The monument was designed by Edinburgh architect Thomas Hamilton Junior, and incorporates Classical references and Masonic symbolism. Built as a tower, it affords views to the surrounding landscape, so loved by Burns. Each year in July wreaths are laid at the monument to commemorate the poet's death.

Following the addition of a statue house and gardens, the Burns Monument Trust acquired Burns Cottage in 1881 for £4,000. They restored the poet's birthplace, later adding a museum to house their increasing collection of Burns manuscripts, artefacts and other Burnsiana – now considered to be the most important Burns collection in the world.

THE GARDENS

'I have some favorite flowers in Spring, among which are the mountain-daisy, the hare-bell, the foxglove, the wild brier-rose, the budding birk, and the hoary hawthorn, that I view and hang over with particular delight.'

(Letter from Robert Burns to Mrs Frances Anna Dunlop, 1 January 1789)

When the monument was built it stood on a relatively small area of ground. Over the years, as more and more visitors came to Alloway, the grounds were gradually expanded. This larger garden and landscape setting is a fitting reminder of the importance of nature in the poetry and songs written by Burns.

THE STATUE HOUSE

The three sandstone sculptures in the statue house depict Tam o' Shanter, Souter Johnie and Nanse Tinnock, the proprietress of an alehouse in Mauchline frequented by Burns and his friends.

They were carved by the self-taught sculptor, James Thom, around 1828. The two male statues originally toured exhibition venues throughout Great Britain, before being displayed in the statue house, specially built in the Monument gardens from profits from the tour.

SOUTER JOHNNIE'S COTTAGE

Main Road, Kirkoswald, South Ayrshire KA19 8HY

John Davidson (1728–1806) was the real-life shoemaker (or souter) upon whom Burns is supposed to have based Tam's favourite drinking companion in *Tam o' Shanter*. Davidson's wife had been in service to Burns's maternal grandfather, and Robert knew the family well. The cottage was built in 1785 and has been furnished in the style of the period. It also contains a fine collection of shoemaking tools.

In another small cottage in the garden are a collection of four life-sized figures from *Tam o' Shanter*, carved by James Thom from sandstone around 1830: Tam, Souter Johnnie, the innkeeper and the innkeeper's wife.

DIRECTIONS: On A77, 4m south of Maybole

OPEN: 25 January and 1 April to 30 September, 11.30-5, Fri-Tues. Admission charge

TEL: 0844 493 2147

DISTANCE: Approx 11 miles (18km) from Robert Burns Birthplace Museum

FACILITIES: Shop; picnic area; family activities; information available in multiple languages; wheelchair access; car parking

BACHELORS' CLUB

Sandgate Street, Tarbolton, South Ayrshire KA5 5RB

In 1779 Burns attended dancing lessons in this seventeenth-century thatched house, and a year later, along with his brother Gilbert and five other young men, he formed a debating club. The 'Bachelors' Club' met in this property and drew up ten rules of membership for the society. In 1781 Burns was initiated into Freemasonry here, in the same upper room where his club met.

Today, the property is a museum to Burns, and is a must-see for any Burns enthusiast. The lower rooms are filled with objects of interest and visitors can also explore the upper room, which has been kept almost as it was in Burns's day.

DIRECTIONS: Off A77, 10m south of Kilmarnock; off A76 at Mauchline; 7½m north-east of Ayr

OPEN: 25 January and 1 April to 30 September, 1-5, Fri-Tues. Admission charge

TEL: 0844 493 2146

DISTANCE: Approx 10 miles (16km) from Robert Burns Birthplace Museum

FACILITIES: Family activities; wheelchair access to ground floor; car parking; guided tours

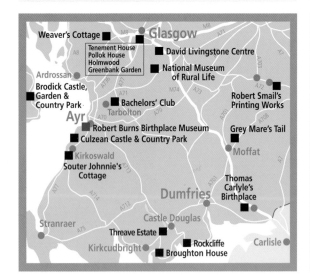

OTHER BURNS SITES

The National Burns Collection is made up of priceless manuscripts, books, relics, art and memorabilia, and is the nation's direct link to Burns. Museums, libraries, archive centres, inns, Masonic lodges, country houses, castles and numerous private collections in Scotland care for a huge range of objects with a particular Burns association. Please visit the website www.burnsscotland.com for details on visiting the many Burns-related sites across Scotland.